THE VEGAN CHINESE COOKBOOK

A Collection of Flavorful Recipes to Help you in your Shift to a Vegan Lifestyle

© Copyright 2020 by EVELYN MOORE All rights reserved.

This document is geared towards providing exact and reliable information in regards to the topic and issue covered. The publication is sold with the idea that the publisher is not required to render accounting, officially permitted, or otherwise, qualified services. If advice is necessary, legal or professional, a practiced individual in the profession should be ordered.

- From a Declaration of Principles which was accepted and approved equally by a Committee of the American Bar Association and a Committee of Publishers and Associations.

In no way is it legal to reproduce, duplicate, or transmit any part of this document in either electronic means or in printed format. Recording of this publication is strictly prohibited and any storage of this document is not allowed unless with written permission from the publisher. All rights reserved.

The information provided herein is stated to be truthful and consistent, in that any liability, in terms of inattention or otherwise, by any usage or abuse of any policies, processes, or directions contained within is the solitary and utter responsibility of the recipient reader. Under no circumstances will any legal responsibility or blame be held against the publisher for any reparation, damages, or monetary loss due to the information herein, either directly or indirectly.

Respective authors own all copyrights not held by the publisher.

The information herein is offered for informational purposes solely, and is universal as so. The presentation of the information is without contract or any type of guarantee assurance.

TABLE OF CONTENTS

Introduction 1

Chapter 1: What it Means to be Vegan 2

Chapter 2: Going Vegan Chinese 5

Chapter 3: Some Common Vegan Ingredients 6

Chapter 4: Breakfast Recipes 8

Chapter 5: Main Course Recipes 17

Chapter 6: Dessert Recipes 33

Conclusion 41

INTRODUCTION

This book contains the basics of entering the vegan lifestyle as well as the knowledge that you can still enjoy eating your favorite cuisines. This book is all about vegan Chinese cuisine.

You may be faced with a dilemma. You love Chinese cuisine; you can't live without your daily pork gua bao. However, for ethical, health, and environmental reasons, you want to make the shift to a healthy vegan lifestyle.

This book highlights the fact that there is no need for you to give up your favorite Chinese dishes. This book features a wealth of recipes ranging from breakfast, main courses, and dessert items. All recipes are vegan. If you want to enjoy noodles, there is no reason why you should not.

This book also delves into the reasons why you should go vegan, what food to eat and avoid, and what food ingredients to stock in your vegan kitchen. As you go through the book, you will find that the ingredients are easily obtainable and the recipes are easy to make.

Essentially, you will realize that you're not giving up the food that you love when you become a vegan. Even if you're a vegan, you can still enjoy various Asian cuisines like Chinese, Japanese, Thai, Indian, and many others. You only need to be mindful of the substitutions.

Thanks for downloading this book, I hope you enjoy it!

CHAPTER 1:
WHAT IT MEANS TO BE VEGAN

Veganism is not only about what you eat, it is also a way of life. Vegans generally choose not to consume eggs, dairy, or any other animal products. Aside from avoiding meat, vegans also adhere to a way of life that seeks to exclude animal cruelty and exploitation, be it from clothing, food, or other purpose.

Veganism Types

Whole-Food Vegans. These vegans prefer a diet rich in whole food like vegetables, fruit, legumes, whole grain, seeds, and nuts.

Dietary Vegans. Also called plant-based eaters, dietary vegans do not eat animal products yet they still use such products like in cosmetics and clothing.

Junk-Food Vegans. These kinds of vegans consume heavily-processed vegan food like fries, vegan meat, desserts, and frozen dinners. Such desserts can include non-dairy cream or Oreo cookies.

Raw-Food Vegans. These vegans only consume food cooked at temperatures below 48°C (118°F). Some of these vegans even consume raw food.

Raw-Food, Low-Fat Vegans. Also considered fruitarians, these vegans do not consume high-fat food like coconuts, avocados, and nuts. They instead eat low-fat fruit like citrus.

Why Go Vegan?

Going vegan is not for everybody. If you cannot avoid animal products, whether eating them or using them, you're off better going on a non-vegan healthy way of living. Vegans normally choose to hold off consuming and using animal products for ethical, health, and environmental reasons.

Ethics. Certain vegans assert that all creatures have the right to freedom and life. Thus, they are averse to ending a living being's life, to drink its milk, wear its skin, or consume its flesh. After all, there are alternatives to animal products. These vegans also are against the physical and psychological stress that creatures may suffer as a result of contemporary farming methods.

Environment. Vegans also avoid animal products due to animal agriculture's environmental impact. Animal agriculture can also result in deforestation, as forest areas are burned for pasture or cropland. Vegans believe the destruction of habitats is a factor in certain animal species' extinction.

Health. People become vegans because the vegan lifestyle offers various health benefits. Plant-based diets can reduce the risk of type 2 diabetes, heart disease, premature death, and certain cancers. Avoiding animal products can also reduce Alzheimer's risk. People also become vegans to avoid the adverse effects related to hormones and antibiotics used in contemporary agriculture.

Food Vegans Eat and Avoid

A standard vegan diet, whether you indulge in a vegan Chinese diet or a vegan Mediterranean diet mostly includes legumes, grains, fruit, and vegetables, and the various dishes created by combining them.

For example, in the vegan Chinese diet, some familiar ingredients include tofu and soy milk. Other food items include lentils, beans, seitan, nuts, tempeh, and seeds.

However, vegans avoid animal origin foods like chicken, meat, shellfish, fish, dairy, eggs, and honey. Vegans also avoid animal by-product ingredients like casein, albumin, carmine, pepsin, gelatin, isinglass, whey, and shellac. In the case of jelly dishes, vegans make their jelly products using seaweed-based agar.

Going vegan is not a boring endeavor. You may even enjoy it. In this book, you are introduced to vegan Chinese cuisine. If you can't get enough of Chinese food and you want to go vegan, you can easily transition into the lifestyle.

If you're interested about going vegan, you'll find the transition can be easy, although you may have to take supplements in order to get your body the right nutritional needs.

CHAPTER 2:
GOING VEGAN CHINESE

Going vegan is not about eating plain vegetables, fruit, grains, and plant-based milks. If you don't know how to combine food properly, your foray into the vegan lifestyle would be boring.

There are others who struggle into becoming vegans, while others find it to be a breeze. There are people that initially become vegetarians, and then they gradually stop eating dairy and eggs. There's no correct way to become a vegan, but it's a good idea to know how people do it. However, you go about your decision, keep in mind the reasons why you go on the lifestyle.

Also remember that you're not giving up flavor. You can still enjoy various cuisines. For example, you can still enjoy Chinese cuisine. You just have to be mindful of substitutions. You can use tempeh, tofu, and bean curd in place of chicken or p0rk. To enliven your Chinese dishes, you can add ingredients like nori and hoisin sauce.

For vegans, there are a lot of Chinese recipes that can be customized for vegans. You can create a vegan Chinese meal at home, and you get to stick to your new lifestyle as you know what you put in the vegan dishes you prepare.

CHAPTER 3:
SOME COMMON VEGAN INGREDIENTS

Chinese cuisine is one of the most popular cuisines around the world. While Chinese cuisine involves ingredients like vegetables and tofu, other ingredients include pork, chicken, duck, and many other meats. This can pose limitations for vegans who want to indulge in Chinese food. There a number of Chinese cuisine ingredients you should keep handy if you're a vegan. To keep things interesting, you need to go beyond the consumption of rice, noodles, vegetables, and tofu.

Roasted or Toasted Seaweed (Yakinori). While yakinori is best known as a wrapper for Japanese sushi, it can also add flavor to Chinese vegan dishes. Because of its paper-like thinness, you can even enjoy yakinori as a snack or you can eat it raw. In vegan Chinese cuisine, you can add shredded yakinori to flavor your dishes.

Bean Curd Sheets. Bean curd sheets can be used interchangeably with tofu. This soybean-based product can be found in Asian grocery stores. The sheets are wiped in a damp cloth prior to cooking or are soaked in water.

Mushrooms. Mushrooms are a staple in most vegan cuisines, not just Chinese. Some of the mushrooms appropriate for vegan Chinese cooking include abalone, straw, and button mushrooms. If you use black mushrooms (dried), soak them in warm water. It is also a good idea to reserve the soaking liquid, which is normally used as a chicken broth substitute.

Walnuts. Protein-rich walnuts are a great meat substitute in vegan Chinese cooking. Walnuts are also known to reduce heart disease risk. Boil the walnuts before using them, as the walnut skin's bitter flavor comes out during stir frying.

Fungi. This means black fungus, which is also known as cloud ears or wood fungus. It is named cloud ears because the fungus expands after soaking, the result resembling clouds. Other edible fungi include golden fungus and white fungus (silver ears or snow ears). After soaking the fungi to soften them, remove the hard fungi piece attached to the woody stem.

Bean Sprouts. Mung bean sprouts' nutritional qualities and crunchy texture make them a popular ingredient in vegan and vegetarian dishes.

Water Chestnuts. Water chestnuts add sweetness and texture to vegan dishes. Fresh chestnuts are best, but you can use the canned variety. When buying fresh water chestnuts, buy more. You can never tell if the chestnut has gone bad if you don't peel it. If you have fewer chestnuts than needed, you can add whole bamboo shoots to your dish.

CHAPTER 4:
BREAKFAST RECIPES

CHINESE PANCAKES WITH HOISIN SAUCE

These pancakes are traditionally served with duck. However, since the recipes in this book are all vegan, the ingredients listed are not animal products. Instead of duck, mushrooms are used instead. As a vegan dish, eggs are not used.

Cooking Time: 10 minutes
Prep Time: 5 minutes
Number of Servings: 6 pancakes
Calories: 138 kcal

Carbohydrates: 16.9g
Protein: 4.8g
Fat: 6.4g

INGREDIENTS:

Hoisin Sauce Ingredients:

- 3 tbsp. soy sauce
- 1 tbsp. white wine vinegar
- 1 tbsp. brown sugar
- ¼ tsp. Chinese five spice
- 1 tsp. peanut butter

Pancake Ingredients:

- 1 tbsp. oil
- 5 c. button mushrooms, sliced
- 2 c. oyster or shiitake mushrooms, sliced
- 6 Chinese pancakes
- 2 spring onions, thinly sliced
- ½ of a cucumber, thinly sliced
- 2 tsp. sesame seeds

DIRECTIONS:

For the hoisin sauce, mix all the sauce ingredients in a small bowl.

In a saucepan, heat a little bit of oil. Put the button and shiitake mushrooms and cook them for 5 minutes on medium heat. Cook to soften them. Pour the hoisin sauce over the mushrooms and cook for five more minutes, or until the sauce becomes glossy and thick.

Serve the cooked mushrooms in the folded pancakes. Garnish with onion and cucumber slices or sticks. Sprinkle the pancakes with sesame seeds.

VEGAN SCALLION PANCAKES

These pancakes are popular among Chinese populations around the world. While commonly consumed as a breakfast food, it can also be a flavorful snack especially when dipped in soy sauce.

Cooking Time: 10 minutes
Prep Time: 10 minutes
Number of Servings: 4 servings
Calories: 136 kcal

Carbohydrates: 17g
Protein: 2g
Fat: 7g

INGREDIENTS:

- 4 c. flour
- 1 ½ c. cold water
- 1 tbsp. vegetable oil
- 1/4 tsp. salt
- ¼ c. oil, for frying
- 2 bunches green onions, sliced

DIRECTIONS:

Mix the water and flour in a bowl until you form a dough. For several minutes, knead the dough on a lightly-floured surface. Return dough to the bowl and cover it. Set the dough aside for around 30 minutes.

Roll the dough into 1/8" thick circular pancakes. On top of each pancake, brush a thin layer of vegan margarine or oil. Sprinkle salt on top. Into the dough, press in some green onions.

Roll the pancakes like in the manner of rolling a cigar. Roll the pancakes again into its circular 1/8" shape, making sure to integrate the onions.

You can divide the dough to make two pancakes. Fry the cakes in 1/4" of oil on medium heat in a skillet. Cook for about 3 minutes each pancake on one side. Flip the pancake and further cook for 2 more minutes. Place the cakes on a plate lined with paper towels.

Season with salt and cut to desired serving pieces. Serve hot with dipping sauce. Enjoy.

GREEN BEAN-TOFU STIR FRY

If you're not only a vegan, but you would like to avoid too many carbohydrates, this is a breakfast dish for you. While seemingly not traditionally a breakfast item, the protein content of this dish can keep you alert and energized for hours.

Cooking Time: 15 minutes
Prep Time: 5 minutes
Number of Servings: 4
Calories: 178.5 kcal

Carbohydrates: 13.75g
Protein: 13.5g
Fat: 9.6g

INGREDIENTS:

- 4 c. green beans, trimmed
- 14 oz. tofu (organic), drained and cubed
- 1 tbsp. extra virgin olive oil
- ¼ c. water or vegetable broth
- 3 tbsp. soy sauce or tamari
- 1 tbsp. maple syrup
- 2 tsp. onion powder
- 1 tbsp. cornstarch
- ½ tsp. red pepper flakes, if desired

DIRECTIONS:

For 8 to 10 minutes, steam the green beans.

Meanwhile, in a non-stick pan on medium, heat and cook the tofu for 5 minutes on one side.

As you cook the tofu, mix until smooth all the sauce ingredients in a small bowl.

Flip the tofu and cook until crispy or cook for 3 to 5 minutes.

Pour the sauce over the tofu. Constantly stir until the sauce thickens.

Turn off the stove. Add the beans. Combine well with the tofu.

Serve with rice or your choice grain.

VEGAN DUMPLINGS

If you're pressed for time in the morning, you can make these dumplings ahead, like the day before. You can easily heat them for a quick vegan Chinese breakfast.

Cooking Time: 15 minutes
Prep Time: 15 minutes
Number of Servings: 4 dumplings
Calories: 139 kcal

Carbohydrates: 24.2g
Protein: 5.5g
Fat: 2g

INGREDIENTS:

- 1 scallion (large), chopped
- 2 tsp. ginger (fresh), chopped
- ½ c. shiitake mushrooms, cooked
- ¼ c. cabbage, shredded
- ½ c. asparagus, chopped finely
- 1 tbsp. soy sauce (reduced sodium)
- 1 tsp. sesame oil
- 12 wonton wrappers (round)

DIRECTIONS:

In a food processor, mix the ingredients, except for the wonton wrappers. Pulse until you get a chunky paste. Remove contents and pour in a medium bowl.

Use a tablespoon to place a proportionate mixture in the wrapper. Press together the edges to form half-moons. Do the same with the rest of the wonton wrappers and the mixture.

If you wish to store the dumplings, do not steam them yet. Freeze them first. Store properly until you're ready to use them.

If you want to eat immediately, steam the dumplings for 10 to 12 minutes.

Serve and enjoy.

BLACK BEAN STIR-FRIED NOODLES

This is a unique spin on a vegan Chinese breakfast. The black bean noodles, with a combination of good carbs and protein, can energize you throughout the day.

Cooking Time: 20 minutes
Prep Time: 25 minutes
Number of Servings: 8
Calories: 162kcal

Carbohydrates: 31.9g
Protein: 6.3g
Fat: 0.7g

INGREDIENTS:

- 16 oz. black bean noodles. Break noodles into 2-inch pieces and cook according to package directions. This helps with mixing in with the vegetables.
- 3 carrots, cut to sticks
- 3 c. button mushrooms, sliced
- 2 c. green beans, cut to 1" pieces
- 1 red onion (large), thinly sliced
- 4 garlic cloves, minced
- 2 vegan sausages, crumbled or cut into 1-cm rings
- 1" ginger knob, minced
- 1 tsp. vegetable oil
- Juice of 1 orange
- 2 tbsp. soy sauce
- 2 tbsp. maple syrup
- 2 tsp. hot sauce like Sriracha
- Salt, to taste

DIRECTIONS:

In a bowl, mix together the maple syrup, orange juice, sriracha, and soy sauce. Set aside.

Heat the oil in a wok. Add the green beans, onions, and carrots. Constantly stir, until the vegetables are crunchy and tender. Add in the mushrooms and cook for 1 minute more.

Add the garlic and ginger. Stir fry for several seconds. Mix in the cooked noodles. Continue to stir fry while stirring frequently with a ladle or tongs. Add the sausage and the soy-sauce orange mixture. Remove from stove. Mix the noodles well. Serve hot. Enjoy.

VEGAN BREAKFAST CONGEE

This Asian rice porridge (congee) is a popular Chinese breakfast item. You can even eat it in cold weather even if it's no longer breakfast time. The edamame, tempeh, and bok choi add a healthy vegan twist.

Cooking Time: 1 hour
Prep Time: 10 minutes
Number of Servings: 4 servings
Calories: 351 kcal
Carbohydrates: 52g
Protein: 15g
Fat: 9g

INGREDIENTS:

- ½ tbsp. sesame oil
- 1 c. white rice (long-grain)
- 2 garlic cloves, minced
- 8 to 10 c. vegetable broth

Topping Ingredients:

- 6 oz. tempeh, cubed
- 1 tsp. paprika
- 1 tbsp. soy sauce
- ½ c. edamame, cooked
- 3 green onions, cut crosswise
- 2 heads bok choi, sliced
- 1 tbsp. black sesame seeds
- 1 tbsp. white sesame seeds
- 1 c. bamboo shoots
- Sriracha sauce
- Soy sauce

DIRECTIONS:

In a medium pot, heat the sesame oil. Add the garlic and the rice and sauté for 1 to 2 minutes. Pour the vegetable broth into the pot and bring to a boil. Reduce heat to simmer. Cover partially and simmer the rice for 1 to 1 ½ hours more. Use a wooden spoon to occasionally stir. If needed, add more broth. The congee should be creamy.

Meanwhile, make the tempeh. In a pan, heat a little sesame oil. Add the soy sauce tempeh, and paprika. Cook until crispy or for 4 minutes. Season with pepper and salt.

To make the bok choi, heat ½ tbsp. water in a lidded pan. For 3 minutes, steam the bok choi. Season with soy sauce.

Ladle the congee in individual bowls. Arrange the toppings. Season with sriracha and soy sauce, if desired. Enjoy.

CHAPTER 5:
MAIN COURSE RECIPES

VEGAN WONTON SOUP

With the flavors of spring, this healthy vegan wonton soup contains a filling of tofu, wood ear mushrooms, and broccoli.

Cooking Time: 5 minutes
Prep Time: 10 minutes
Number of Servings: 2 servings
Calories: 493 kcal

Carbohydrates: 76g
Protein: 16g
Fat: 13g

INGREDIENTS:

- ½ c. wood ear mushrooms, soak in water for 10 minutes, chop to pieces
- 1 broccoli head (small), cut to pieces
- ¼ box tofu (fresh), chopped
- 1 tsp. sesame oil
- 1 tsp. salt
- ¼ tsp. white pepper
- 20 pcs. wonton wrappers
- 4 c. water

Serving Bowl Seasonings:

- 1 tbsp. scallion, chopped
- ½ tsp. garlic, minced
- ½ tsp. salt
- ½ tsp. soy sauce (light)
- 1 tsp. sesame oil
- 1 pc. Nori (dried)

DIRECTIONS:

Put the mushrooms, tofu, and broccoli in a large bowl. Add the salt, pepper, and oil. Combine to mix well.

Place a spoonful of the filling in each wonton wrapper, properly sealing the edges. Boil water in a large pot. Add the dried nori, soy sauce, garlic, salt, spring onions, and sesame oil. Place wonton's into the boiling water and continue to cook over a medium heat for 3 to 4 minutes.

Serve into bowl and garnish with chopped scallions and serve immediately.

LO MEIN

You can use any vegan-friendly ingredients you can find in your refrigerator. This dish is an excellent main dish or side course. If you desire, you can add some cut-up bean curd sheets or roasted seaweed. Buckwheat noodles are best as they fill you up and energize you for hours.

Cooking Time: 15 minutes
Prep Time: 10 minutes
Number of Servings: 2 servings
Calories: 178 kcal

Carbohydrates: 30g
Protein: 5g
Fat: 4g

INGREDIENTS:

- 6 oz. to 8 oz. soba noodles (vegan). You can also use similar noodles like brown rice-based pad thai noodles

Sauce Ingredients:

- 1 to 2 tsp. sesame oil
- 3 tbsp. soy sauce
- 1 tbsp. ginger, minced
- 1 tsp. sugar

Vegetable Ingredients:

- ½ of onion (small), chopped finely
- 1 green chili, sliced thinly
- 4 cloves garlic, chopped finely
- 2 to 3 c. of your choice vegetables like mushrooms, sliced bell peppers, snow peas, broccoli, chopped spinach, julienned carrots, or chard
- Black pepper, salt, and/or red pepper flakes, to taste

DIRECTIONS:

Cook noodles according to package instructions.

In a bowl, combine and mix well together the sesame oil, soy sauce, ginger, and sugar. Set aside.

In a large skillet on medium, heat oil. Add the garlic, onions, bell peppers, chili, and mushrooms. Cook for around 4 minutes while occasionally stirring.

Add the broccoli and other vegetables. Add a dash of black pepper and salt and cook for 3 to 4 minutes more or until the mushrooms turn a golden brown color.

Add the cooked noodles and sauce to the skillet and toss the ingredients to combine. If needed, adjust the heat.

Add a sprinkle of red pepper flakes and ground pepper. Serve and enjoy.

FRIED VEGAN RICE

The fried rice is so easy to make. You only need a few ingredients. You can eat it on its own or you can pair it with tofu or vegetables of your choice.

Cooking Time: 20 minutes
Prep Time: 5 minutes
Number of Servings: 2 servings
Calories: 556 kcal

Carbohydrates: 94.2g
Protein: 11.6g
Fat: 15.3g

INGREDIENTS:

- 1 c. rice, raw
- ½ c. corn kernels
- ½ c. peas
- 1 or 2 tbsp. extra virgin olive oil
- 2 cloves garlic, chopped
- ½ of an onion, chopped
- 1 carrot, diced
- 2 tbsp. tamari or soy sauce

DIRECTIONS:

Cook the rice. It's best to cook it the day before.

Cook the corn kernels and peas according to package instructions, if you are using frozen or fresh peas. If you are using canned corn kernels and peas, you don't need to cook.

In a skillet or wok, add the onion, garlic, and carrot. Cook for 2 minutes on medium-high heat. Add the corn kernels and peas and cook for 2 minutes more.

Add the soy sauce or tamari and rice. Cook until the rice is heated through, or for about 2 to 3 minutes.

BROCCOLI AND CHICKPEAS

If you're a vegan who wants to enjoy a home-cooked Chinese meal on a busy night, this is perfect for you. It's easy to prepare and you get your daily dose of protein with this flavorful dish.

Cooking Time: 20 minutes
Prep Time: 10 minutes
Number of Servings: 2 servings
Calories: 516 kcal

Carbohydrates: 97g
Protein: 21g
Fat: 5g

INGREDIENTS:

Sauce Ingredients:

- ¼ c. sugar
- 2 to 3 tbsp. rice vinegar
- 2 tbsp. apple cider vinegar
- 1 ½ tbsp. ketchup
- 2 tsp. soy sauce
- ½ tsp. garlic powder
- 2 tbsp. water

Vegetables:

- 1 tsp. oil
- 3 garlic cloves, chopped finely
- ½ of a red bell pepper (large), sliced thinly
- ½ of a green bell pepper, sliced thinly
- 1 c. broccoli florets (small)
- 15 oz. chickpeas or 1 ½ c. chickpeas, cooked
- Salt and black pepper, to taste
- Cayenne pepper, to taste

Thickeners:

- 2 tsp. cornstarch
- 2 tbsp. water

DIRECTIONS:

In a small bowl, mix together the sauce ingredients. Set aside.

In a large skillet on medium-high, heat the oil. Add the garlic until it becomes translucent, or cook for 2 minutes.

Mix in the peppers. Cover the pot for 2 minutes. Mix in the broccoli. Cover the pot and cook for 1 minute.

Add the sauce ingredients, chickpeas. Season with salt, cayenne pepper, and black pepper. Turn down the heat to medium. Cover and let cook for 10 more minutes. If you still need a sweet-sour flavor, add more sugar or salt.

Mix together the water and the cornstarch, and add the mix to the pan. Cover and allow the sauce to thicken for 2 to 3 minutes.

Remove from heat. Garnish with red pepper flakes, scallions, and sesame seeds if desired. Serve with cooked rice. Enjoy.

TOFU AND CASHEW STIR FRY

This dish is a favorite in most Asian cuisines. It is easy and quick to prepare and you can enjoy it as a weeknight meal.

Cooking Time: 20 minutes
Prep Time: 10 minutes
Number of Servings: 2 servings
Calories: 319 kcal

Carbohydrates: 32g
Protein: 14g
Fat: 16g

INGREDIENTS:

Stir Fry Ingredients:

- 1/3 c. cashews (unsalted or raw), roasted
- 1 tsp. oil
- 4 garlic cloves, chopped finely
- 4 red chilies (dried), broken
- 1/2 inch ginger, chopped finely
- 1/3 c. onion, chopped
- 7 oz. to 8 oz. tofu (firm or extra firm), pressed and cubed
- ½ of a bell pepper (green), chopped or ¾ cup broccoli, chopped or sliced thinly
- ¼ tsp. white or black pepper, or both

Sauce Ingredients:

- 1 tbsp. soy sauce
- 2 tsp. rice wine vinegar
- 3 tbsp. or more hoisin sauce (vegan)
- ¼ c. sugar
- ¼ tsp. sesame oil (toasted)
- ¼ c. water or vegetable broth

DIRECTIONS:

In a skillet on medium, heat the oil. Add the chilies and cashews and cook until the cashews on most sides have a gold color. Frequently stir.

Add the ginger and garlic. Combine well and cook until translucent or for 2 minutes.

Add the vegetables, onion, and a pinch of salt. Turn up the heat to medium-high. Cook for up to 3 minutes. Stir frequently. Add the black pepper and tofu and cook for 2 to 3 minutes more.

In a small bowl, mix the sauce ingredients well. Add to the skillet. Cook for one minute. Season if needed.

For a few minutes, simmer the mixture until the sauce slightly thickens. Serve over cooked brown/white rice.

SPICY ORANGE PEPPERS AND TOFU

This is an excellent weeknight dinner dish. The tofu mixes well with the zesty orange glaze and the sweet and sour flavor.

Cooking Time: 20 minutes
Prep Time: 20 minutes
Number of Servings: 2 servings
Calories: 236 kcal

Carbohydrates: 28g
Protein: 8g
Fat: 9g

INGREDIENTS:

- 2 tbsp. water (warm)
- ¼ c. water, for more sauce and for thinning
- 2 to 3 tsp. cornstarch. Add more starch for a thicker glaze and sauce
- 2 tbsp. rice vinegar
- 2 tbsp. soy sauce or liquid aminos
- 2 tbsp. maple syrup or 1 tbsp. sugar (raw)
- Zest of 1 small orange or clementine
- 1 to 2 tbsp. Asian hot chili paste
- 1 tbsp. oil
- Juice of 1 orange (about 1/3 c.)
- 2 to 3 garlic cloves, finely slice/chopped
- 7 oz. firm tofu, cubed and drained of excess moisture
- ½ bell pepper (green), sliced thinly

DIRECTIONS:

Whisk the 2 tbsp. warm water and cornstarch in a bowl. Add rice vinegar, soy sauce, hot chili paste, maple, orange juice, and zest. Mix and set aside.

In a large wok or non-stick pan on medium-high, heat oil. Add the tofu and cook for about 6 to 8 minutes and the sides are browned. Add the bell peppers and garlic. Cook for half a minute.

Add the sauce. If you want a thinner sauce, add more water. Cook for 2 to 4 minutes or until the sauce begins to bubble. Reduce heat and cover the pan. Cook for 2 more minutes.

Serve with rice. Enjoy.

SHU MAI WITH ZUCCHINI AND BROCCOLI

You can serve this as an appetizer, side dish, or as a snack. If you want this as a vegan main course, you can eat more. The dumplings are best served with hoisin sauce and beet slices.

Cooking Time: 20 minutes
Prep Time: 45 minutes
Number of Servings: 5 servings
Calories: 156 kcal

Carbohydrates: 27g
Protein: 3g
Fat: 3g

INGREDIENTS:

Wrapper Ingredients:

- 1 c. all-purpose flour
- Warm water
- ¼ tsp. salt, to taste
- Cornstarch
- 1 tsp. oil

Filling Ingredients:

- ½ c. zucchini, chopped
- ½ c. broccoli (small), chopped
- 1 tsp. sesame oil
- 1 tsp. canola oil
- 2 tsp. hoisin sauce
- ½ tsp. chili flakes
- ½ tsp. agave syrup or raw sugar
- 1 tbsp. or more garlic, chopped

DIRECTIONS:

In a bowl, combine the flour, salt, and ½ tsp. of cornstarch.

Use oil to grease your hand. Add warm water gradually until you form a dough. Knead for several minutes until it is elastic and does not stick.

Cover the dough with a towel. Let the dough rest for 30 minutes to one hour.

Divide the dough into small balls. Roll out each ball until they are flattened. Alternatively, you can roll out the big ball and cut circle or square shapes.

During the rolling out process, you may want to use cornstarch for dusting for easy handling and to prevent stickiness.

To store the wrappers if you will not use immediately, dust with cornstarch and refrigerate in an air-tight container.

To cook the filling, heat the canola oil. Add chili flakes and garlic and cook for a few seconds on medium. Toss in the zucchini and the broccoli. Cook for 3 to 4 minutes.

Add hoisin sauce, sugar, salt, and sesame oil. Mix thoroughly. Cover and cook for 3 to 4 minutes more.

Add more spices and seasonings, if desired. Allow to cool.

Assembly Directions:

Roll a piece of dough into a 3-inch circle. Place the wrapper on your palm. Add some filling on the wrapper. Push down the shu mai gradually in the hole between your index finger and your thumb to wrap the filling with the wrapper.

Push the wrapper's edges inward. Make small folds on the top edges to cover. It should resemble a pouch. You may want to leave some of the filling uncovered. If needed, use water to seal the wrapper folds.

Steam the shu mai until the wrapper becomes translucent, or for 7 to 10 minutes.

Serve with hoisin dipping sauce and beet slices.

FRITTERS WITH SEAWEED AND MUSHROOMS

You may want to prepare this dish ahead of time, since it takes long to press the tofu and soak the mushrooms. You can eat this as an accompaniment to you main vegan dish.

Cooking Time: 20 minutes
Prep Time: 4 hours
Number of Servings: 10 servings
Calories: 491g

Carbohydrates: 2.6g
Protein: 10.3g
Fat: 48.7g

INGREDIENTS:

Fritter Ingredients:

- 1 oz. Chinese mushrooms, dried
- 23 oz. bean curd, firm
- 2 to 3 cubes Chinese bean curd (fermented)
- 2 shallots (large), peeled
- 1 oz. spring onions
- ⅞ oz. coriander or cilantro (fresh)
- Sea salt
- ½ tsp. white pepper, finely ground
- ½ tsp. Japanese seven spice powder, or toasted sesame seeds and a small amount of chili flakes
- 1/60 oz. nori (dried seaweed), shredded
- Oil, for frying

Dipping Sauce Ingredients:

- 4 ¾ tsp. sea salt
- ¾ tsp. white pepper, finely ground
- ½ c. lime juice
- Fresh lime wedges

DIRECTIONS:

Rinse the mushrooms in hot water. Soak for around 2 hours or until the mushrooms become hydrated and expand.

Use paper towels to dry the tofu blocks. Wrap the tofu and place the tofu on a tray. Weigh the tofu down and refrigerate for 2 hours.

Afterwards, place the tofu in a bowl. Use a potato masher to mash the tofu until you get a rough paste.

Drain the mushrooms and remove excess water. Discard the stems. Dice the remaining mushrooms. Mince the spring onions and shallots. Chop the cilantro.

In the bowl with tofu, add the fermented bean curd, mushrooms, coriander, and spring onion. Season with the white pepper, the seven-spice powder, and 1 tsp. salt. Add the nori, and add seasonings to taste. Refrigerate for 2 more hours.

Shape the mixture into 1" balls and fry them until the balls are a pale gold color and the exterior is set. Drain on paper towels. You can also fry them twice if you want crunchier fritters.

For the dipping sauce, mix the pepper and the salt. Divide among shallow, small balls. Add the lime juice to form a sauce.

Arrange the tofu fritters on a serving plate. Serve with the dipping sauce and garnish with the lime wedges.

WATER CHESTNUT AND BEAN SPROUT STIR FRY

This wonderful, nutty main course can be eaten alone or together with other flavorful dishes like fried vegan rice. This can be a wonderful dinner on a cold night.

Cooking Time: 35 minutes
Prep Time: 20 minutes
Number of Servings: 4 servings
Calories: 308kcal
Carbohydrates: 51g
Protein: 14.7g
Fat: 9g

INGREDIENTS:

- 10 ½ oz. water chestnut
- 10 pcs. button mushrooms
- 1 pc. red Bell pepper
- 1 pc. yellow Bell Pepper
- 1 head broccoli
- 2 heads Bok Choy
- 1 c. bean sprouts
- 5 stalks spring onion, chopped
- 2 tbsp. soy sauce
- 1 tsp. black pepper
- 2 tbsp. cooking oil

DIRECTIONS:

Place the water chestnuts in a pressure cooker with water. Cook for at least 8 whistles. Let it rest for several seconds or until the cooker naturally releases pressure.

Remove the black skin. Cut the chestnuts into half.

In a wok, add the yellow and red peppers. Stir fry until they are slightly crunchy yet soft. Add the bok choy and broccoli. Continue to stir fry until they are cooked. Stir in the mushrooms and continue to cook until moisture is removed.

Mix in the bean sprouts and the water chestnuts. Continue to stir fry for 5 minutes more. Season with soy sauce, black pepper, and salt.

Sprinkle some of the chopped spring onion on top. Serve hot and enjoy.

CHAPTER 6:
DESSERT RECIPES

ALMOND PUDDING

The best almonds for use in this recipe are south Chinese almonds, which are sweet and large. Aside from the making of almond pudding, Chinese almonds can be used to make savory soups like herbal soups and watercress soups.

Cooking Time: 5 minutes
Prep Time: 10 minutes
Number of Servings: 6 servings
Calories: 306.58 kcal

Carbohydrates: 24.48g
Protein: 9.49g
Fat: 21.32g

INGREDIENTS:

- 2 c. almond milk (unsweetened), add extra ¼ c.
- 3 tbsp. agave syrup
- 2 tsp. agar-agar powder. If you desire a softer texture, use 1 ½ tsp. instead.
- 6 oz. almonds (blanched) or Chinese dried almonds (dried apricot kernels)
- 11 oz. raspberries (fresh)
- 3 oz. walnuts, removed from shell

DIRECTIONS:

In a food processor, blend the Chinese almonds and almond milk until a creamy, smooth consistency is achieved.

In a bowl, whisk together thoroughly the agar-agar powder and the ¼ c. almond milk.

In a pot, combine the agar-agar blend and almond mixture. Add the agave syrup. Bring the mixture to boil. Simmer on low. Stir until both the agave and the agar-agar have melted. Turn off heat.

Through a fine strainer or sieve, pass the pudding mixture into a bowl to remove solid almond pieces.

Pour the almond-agar mixture into 6 small bowls or pudding bowls.

Refrigerate for 1 to 2 hours or when the pudding has set.

Remove pudding from mold.

Roughly chop or process in a blender the walnuts.

Serve the pudding with raspberries and the ground nuts.

MANGO PUDDING

Instead of using regular milk or whipping cream, this recipe calls for the use of plant-based coconut milk. Coconut milk brings out the mango's taste. It also makes the pudding richer.

Cooking Time: 5 minutes
Prep Time: 15 minutes
Number of Servings: 3 to 4
Calories: 259 kcal

Carbohydrates: 33g
Protein: 4g
Fat: 15g

INGREDIENTS:

- 1 packet (3 tsp) seaweed-based gelatin
- 2 mangoes (medium to large), ripe
- 1/3 c. white sugar
- ½ c. hot water
- 1 c. coconut milk

DIRECTIONS:

Scoop out the mango pulp. Place the mango pieces in a blender or food processor. Blitz until you achieve a smooth puree. Leave mango in the blender/processor.

Heat the water in a saucepan until boiling, and remove from heat. As you stir the water with a fork or whisk, sprinkle the gelatin over the water surface and briskly stir to prevent lumps.

Add the sugar to the gelatin/hot water mix. Stir to dissolve. Add the sugar-gelatin-water mix to the mango in the blender/food processor. Pour in the coconut milk. Briefly blitz all the ingredients until they are thoroughly combined.

Pour into dessert cups or bowls. Refrigerate for at least 2 hours. Serve and enjoy. You may add fresh fruit.

BERRIES AND COCO WATER JELLY

Jelly desserts are not only common in China. They are also common across Asia. The agar-agar powder is derived from agar, which has no sugar, is high in fiber, and has no calories, fat, or carbohydrates. Agar is also gluten-free.

Cooking Time: 10 minutes
Prep Time: 10 minutes
Number of Servings: 12 servings
Calories: 99 kcal

Carbohydrates: 22.1g
Protein: 1.8g
Fat: 1g

INGREDIENTS:

Jelly Ingredients:

- 6 c. coconut water
- 3 tbsp. agar-agar powder. If you want a softer texture, use 2 ½ tbsp. agar-agar powder
- 2 ½ tbsp. stevia
- 7 oz. blueberries, washed
- 7 oz. raspberries, washed
- 9 oz. strawberries, washed and cut into quarters
- 1 oz. goji berries, dried

Garnish Ingredients:

- A handful of strawberries, washed
- A handful of raspberries, washed
- A handful of blueberries, washed
- A handful of goji berries, dried

DIRECTIONS:

Mix together the berries and divide them among 12 small bowls or pudding molds (non-stick). Fill each bowl to half-full.

In a pot, combine the agar-agar powder and coconut water. Whisk to thoroughly combine.

Bring to boil and simmer on low. Stir until the agar-agar has thickened and melted. Turn off heat.

Pour the agar-agar mix into the berry-filled containers.

Chill for at least two hours.

Use a smooth-edged knife around the sides to remove the jelly from the individual containers.

Place some extra berries on the side of each serving. Enjoy.

LYCHEE SORBET

Lychee is the main ingredient in this dessert. Not only is it delicious and refreshing, it is also easy to make.

Cooking Time: 10 minutes
Prep Time: 10 minutes
Number of Servings: 4 servings
Calories: 24.77 kcal

Carbohydrates: 6.13g
Protein: 0.05g
Fat: 0.05g

INGREDIENTS:

- 2 tbsp. agave syrup
- 2 cans (20 oz. each) lychees or 19 oz. lychee flesh (fresh)
- Small sprig of fresh mint leaves (optional)45

DIRECTIONS:

Combine the agave syrup and the lychees in a food processor. Blend until you achieve a smooth texture.

Pour contents into a sturdy container and freeze for at least 8 hours. Use a fork to check occasionally and see if the right consistency is achieved. Once properly set, remove the lychee mix and divide among serving containers.

Garnish with mint leaves. Serve and enjoy.

CHINESE FIVE-SPICE PEANUTS

In Chinese culture, peanuts represent fertility and longevity. They are also great as snacks.

Cooking Time: 20 minutes
Prep Time: 20 minutes
Number of Servings: 6 to 8 servings

Calories: 266 kcal
Carbohydrates: 15g
Protein: 9g
Fat: 21g

INGREDIENTS:

- 2 c. peanuts (skinless), unsalted
- ¼ c. brown sugar
- 2 tbsp. vegan butter
- 1 tbsp. light corn syrup
- ½ tsp. five-spice powder

DIRECTIONS:

Use wax paper or foil to line a baking sheet. You can also use non-stick cooking spray.

In a small saucepan over medium heat, melt the vegan butter, corn syrup, and brown sugar. Stir until the sugar is dissolved. Add the five-spice powder and bring the mixture to boil.

Boil the mixture for a few minutes without stirring. When you achieve the 'soft ball' state, remove the pan from the heat. Stir in the nuts.

On the baking sheet, spread out the mixture. Allow the peanuts to harden and break into pieces. Store the peanut pieces in an air-tight canister.

WALNUT COOKIES

These crunchy cookies are crumbly, sweet, and packed with the walnuts' earthy flavor. These cookies are best served warm.

Cooking Time: 20 minutes
Prep Time: 30 minutes
Number of Servings: 18 cookies
Calories: 164kcal
Carbohydrates: 20.4g
Protein: 2.5g
Fat: 8.6g

INGREDIENTS:

- ½ c. walnuts
- ¼ c. walnuts, for topping
- 2 c. flour (all-purpose)
- ½ c. coconut oil
- ½ c. coconut sugar
- ¼ c. sugar, granulated
- 1 tbsp. flaxseed (ground), plus 2 ½ tbsp. water
- 1 tsp. salt
- ¼ tsp. baking powder
- ¼ tsp. baking soda
- 2 tbsp. soy milk
- 1 tbsp. maple syrup

DIRECTIONS:

Mix together the flaxseed and water to make the flax egg. To thicken, set aside for 5 minutes.

In a preheated 300°F oven, toast the walnuts for 5 minutes. Afterwards, transfer to walnuts into a food processor, and blend until the walnuts are finely chopped.

Mix together the sugar, coconut oil, flax egg, and salt. Add in the ground walnuts and flour. Stir until combined well.

Form the walnut dough into discs. Arrange on a baking sheet lined with parchment paper.

In the center of each cookie, place a walnut half.

Mix together the maple syrup and soy milk. Brush gently each of the cookies with the syrup-milk mixture.

In a 360°F oven, bake the cookies until golden brown or bake for 17 to 20 minutes. Serve and enjoy.

CONCLUSION

I'd like to thank you and congratulate you for transiting my lines from start to finish.

I hope this book was able to help you to know more about what it means to be a vegan, as well as let you know more about vegan Chinese cooking, especially the recipes and the ingredients to cook such dishes.

The next step is to formulate your meal plan and prepare the list of ingredients to buy, so you can enjoy the vegan Chinese culinary experience.

I wish you the best of luck!

Made in the USA
Monee, IL
01 March 2022